Living in SYDNEY

Robert Moore

Macdonald

Series and book editor: Polly Dunnett
Series designer: Sally Boothroyd
Book designer: Danuta Trebus
Picture researcher: Caroline Mitchell
Production controller: Marguerite Fenn

Consultant: Robert Mackie

A MACDONALD BOOK
© Macdonald & Company 1986
First published in Great Britain in 1986
by Macdonald & Company (Publishers) Ltd
London and Sydney
A BPCC plc company
All rights reserved
Made and printed by
Henri Proost, Belgium

Macdonald & Company (Publishers) Ltd
Greater London House
Hampstead Road
London NW1 7QX

The author would like to thank Jo Blackman,
Joyce Saalmans and the Osgoods for their
help in the preparation of this book.

Cover picture: Sydney Harbour Bridge from
the north shore. Harbourside homes are in
great demand and the older mansions are
now outnumbered by blocks of flats, or
'home units'.

Endpapers: Looking south across the
harbour. From left to right you can see the
botanical gardens, Opera House, Harbour
Bridge and docks. In the distance is Botany
Bay.

Title page: Sydney is built around a great
harbour by a great ocean. You can fish from
rocks high above the sea, or in peaceful inlets
like this.

Contents: There are many classes of racing
yachts that race on Sydney harbour each
Saturday, from the famous six-metre craft
down to simple dinghys like these for young
people.

Artist
Raymond Turvey 42–43

Photographic sources
Key to position of pictures:
(T) top, (C) centre, (R) right, (L) left, (B) bottom

All-Sport: 23B
Australian Tourist Commission: 29T, 39TR & B
Barnaby's Picture Library: 13
BBC Hulton Picture Library: 11B
Mary Evans Picture Library: 10, 11T
Greg Evans Picture Library: Cover
Chris Fairclough: 27L, 28B
Robert Harding Picture Library: 23T, 27T, 40-41
Hutchinson Library: 30T, 37T
Christine Osborne: Contents page, 8, 16B, 18T,
    19T, 20T, 21B, 27R, 28T, 30B, 32T, 33T, 34-35,
    35T & B, 36T & B, 38
Popperfoto: 12, 12-13
Fiona Pragoff: Title page, 9T, C & B, 14-15T, 16T,
    16-17T, 17B, 20B, 21T, 22, 24, 25, 31T, 32B,
    32-33B, 40, 44
Spectrum Colour Library: 15, 18B, 19B, 41T
Andrew Varley: 22-23
ZEFA: endpapers, 14-15B, 28B, 29B, 31B, 38-39

BRITISH LIBRARY CATALOGUING IN PUBLICATION DATA

Moore, Robert, 1942–
    Living in Sydney.—(City life)
    1. Sydney (N.S.W.)—Social life and
    customs—Juvenile literature
    I. Title   II. Series
    994.4'1063

    ISBN 0-356-10328-5

Contents

The good life – Sydney-style

In Australia, a bigger proportion of the population lives in cities than in any other country in the world. The majority of Australia's 15 million people live in a handful of big cities on the fertile east and south coasts. They do not live in crowded city centres, but in sprawling suburbs. Most families have their own single-storey house on its own block of land in a network of similar streets.

The outdoor life

The Australian way of life is carried on outdoors most of the year with picnics, barbecues, swimming and all kinds of sport. Nowhere is this way of life lived with such gusto as in Sydney. Here the harbour, the beaches and above all the warm, temperate climate encourage the outdoor life and give it a character all its own. Whether or not they live close to the harbour or the beach, Sydneysiders make it their business to enjoy themselves.

Land and water

A glance at a map of Sydney shows an astonishingly grand and complex pattern of land and water. Sydney has been formed by its harbour. This was once a deep river valley, which flooded to form the intricate system of

inlets and headlands that now both join and separate the many suburbs of Sydney. In modern times, the harbour has made Sydney a great port and provided its people with a beautiful setting for the city as well as a spectacular playground for sailing and boating of all kinds.

Getting about Sydney without a car can be very difficult because of the way the harbour and its offshoots split everything up, and because the suburban life takes up so much space. Many families who are lucky enough to live around the harbour have two cars for work, school, shopping and pleasure. In the less attractive and less prosperous inland suburbs, which spread westward to the mountains, public transport is stretched to the limit. Here two cars are almost a necessity, and yet some families can barely afford one. However there is so much natural beauty in and around the huge area we call Sydney that everyone can get out into the sunshine to the beach, harbour or bush not only at weekends but before, after and even during working hours.

A brief winter interrupts this schedule of work and play. The average winter temperature is 12°C, and occasionally the city is hit by terrific storms that uproot trees and wash away the sand from beaches. Throughout

Above: Where else but in Sydney would you find an ice-cream boat? This scene is typical of hundreds of sheltered marinas around Sydney, where simple pleasures are given serious practical consideration.

Left: Eating out in Sydney very often means exactly that – lunching or dining outside. There is nothing elaborate about this average Sydney 'beer garden', just local wine and beer with good cheap food in a relaxed atmosphere. At a place like this favourite dishes are grilled steak or fish, pizzas and pasta.

Below: Not everyone in Sydney has a cabinned motor launch; not everyone has a boat. But the sheltered harbour waters and rivers belong to everyone and simple row boats, like the one this family has, are easy to hire.

the year, however, the people of Sydney enjoy an average of nearly seven hours sunshine a day, and they make the most of it.

Inland Sydney

Today, a high proportion of Sydney's 3½ million inhabitants, many of them recent immigrants, live in new suburbs as much as 40 kilometres from the city centre. But even though it has grown so much in the last 20 years, Sydney still provides its own unique way of life. It is taken for granted that everyone has the right to expect an equal share in the riches the city is blessed with.

Left: The back-yard suburban barbecue is an every-day event, not a special occasion. The ingredients are simple: chops, sausages, steak, hamburgers, baked potatoes and salad. Once cooked, the meal may be eaten outside or in. The barbecue meal suits the informality of Australian life and of course, especially in Sydney, the climate.

Early history

Australia has been inhabited for perhaps 40 000 years by its native, or aboriginal, people. They migrated from the north when Australia was still joined to Asia. Gradually they spread through the land, and evolved a life perfectly adapted to the meagre resources of food and water.

Discovery and settlement

From about the 16th century, the Europeans began to explore what was for them the far and unknown side of the world, believing there to be a Great South Land. Several voyages touched on the shores of Australia before an Englishman, Captain James Cook, sailed up the fertile east coast and 'discovered' what he named Botany Bay (south of modern Sydney) in 1770. He claimed all these lands for Great Britain.

But Sydney began ingloriously as a penal colony. The British Government decided to use Botany Bay as a dumping ground for the overflow of criminals that had been created by the harsh laws of the new industrial Britain. Lord Sydney was in charge of the venture and he appointed Captain Arthur

Phillip first governor of the colony. Phillip was sent out on his nine month sea journey with about 600 convicts and a garrison of half as many officers, wives and ordinary soldiers. On their arrival, Phillip saw immediately that Cook's Botany Bay was not suitable for settlement. But to the north, inside the great harbour that Cook had seen but not explored, Phillip found a sheltered cove which offered deep anchorage and fresh water. The First Fleet, as it was later known, disembarked here on 26 January 1788, and named their landing place Sydney Cove.

They quickly came up against difficulties. The source of fresh water, known as the Tank Stream, became muddied as the vegetation was cleared. Nothing would grow in the hard soil, and the few animals they had brought were lost in the bush. The Europeans and the Aborigines, failing completely to understand each other's customs, soon clashed.

Despite Governor Phillip's best efforts, his wretched little community, 20 000 kilometres from home, nearly starved before the Second Fleet arrived, two years later, with essential

Below: Sydney in 1803. In the background, buildings cluster round and up the slopes from the head of Sydney Cove, where Circular Quay was later established. On the right is the steep slope of the Rocks. The first settlement was known as The Camp for some years and the first governor's house was made of canvas. Later, when groups of convicts were set to making bricks and quarrying the local sandstone, the Sydney Town of this view came into being.

supplies. On Phillip's return to England they were left without strong leadership, and things went from bad to worse as the officers tyrannized the colony.

Wool and prosperity

From 1810, however, under Governor Macquarie, a great programme of town planning and public building was begun. Lachlan Macquarie laid down the basis of the present city. Whaling had been the first industry but now farming was beginning to look the most likely way for the colony to support itself. The pioneer in this enterprise was the flamboyant adventurer John Macarthur (who was a thorn in the side of one governor after another). Then, when the Blue Mountains, which had always seemed to be impassable, were finally crossed in 1813, vast new sheep-grazing grounds were opened up on the other side. Soon Sydney wool was being sold profitably in Europe. The colony expanded as new settlers and freed convicts took up grants of land or simply rode out and took land as 'squatters'.

During this period the convicts themselves were cruelly worked in chain gangs. At the same time, the Aborigines gradually retreated before firearms and diseases. The new inhabitants wanted to forget these people and, proud of their new town and colony, were also rapidly becoming ashamed of the convicts. The shipment of convicts was stopped in 1847.

19th century Sydney

So ended the first, and most colourful, phase of the history of Sydney. The second began with the tremendous influx of settlers who came – mainly from Britain and Ireland as before – with the Australian gold rush of the 1850s. This brought new prosperity to Sydney. The city grew rapidly as manufacturing industries were set up. Sydney was becoming a great port based on wool, and also wheat.

Parliamentary government began in 1855, dominated by the wealthy, adventurous successors to Macarthur who had opened up the land and were now building palatial houses by the harbour. Debates raged about rights to the rich grazing lands of the old squatters and the new 'free selectors'. A fine university was built, and by the 1880s there were trains and trams. Sydney had acquired

the solid look of a 19th century English city.

All this time, the separate colonies of Australia were moving towards forming a federation of states and a new nation, Australia. They were all hit by the Great Depression of the 1890s when wool and wheat prices plummeted. But Sydney kept on building grandly, confident of its future, and by the late 1890s it had become the centre of a proud new spirit of nationalism.

Left: Until 1870, Sydney was a garrison town. For a time, the military barracks that Governor Macquarie built were the largest in the British Empire. In this picture officers and wives promenade along the George Street of 1820 as if it were Regent Street in London – which was seven months away by sailing ship.

Below: Another part of George Street in the 1880's, with the newly built town hall in the background. The streets of Sydney were admired as broad and straight by visitors from abroad. They were amazed to find such imposing stone buildings, elegant shops, and gas lamps in this colonial outpost. Not only the buildings the proud colonists erected, but the heavy woollen clothes they wore, and the mutton and potatoes they ate, were the same as if they lived in damp and foggy London.

The 20th century

In 1901, the separate colonies of Australia finally joined together, or federated. They formed one, new, independent nation of Australia, and Sydney, with a population of nearly 500 000, became the capital of New South Wales.

But for the next fifty years of its history the city itself experienced very little of the drama and excitement of earlier days. Helped by the growth of the railway network, suburban Sydney quietly established itself, and the events that most affected Sydney took place abroad – two world wars and the crash of the American stock market in 1929.

World War I

World War I did not threaten the security of Australia, yet it meant a great deal to Australians. It gave them the chance to prove their nationhood in the service of Britain, which was still regarded as the mother country. Australian soldiers, all volunteers, displayed extraordinary courage – in 1915, with the New Zealanders at Gallipoli against the Turks, and later in Palestine and France. Fighting for others, Australia lost a far higher proportion of its population than any other country.

The Depression and World War II

The world-wide Great Depression which followed the crash of 1929 reminded Sydney (and the whole country) that, just as in the 1890s, it was totally at the mercy of world market prices. The hardship and poverty endured by a great many people in Sydney was as severe as in any big city in America or Britain.

But the true optimism of the people triumphed. At this very time the building of the long-dreamed-of Harbour Bridge was undertaken, and its construction provided badly needed jobs for thousands of workers.

In World War II, Australians again went overseas to fight, at first in the North African desert, but then much closer to home in the jungles of Malaya and New Guinea. This time Australia was directly involved and, on one occasion, three Japanese miniature submarines even succeeded in getting into Sydney harbour.

Above: Crowds pour over the Harbour Bridge after its ceremonial opening on 19 March 1932. The Bridge joined the two halves of Sydney together at last.

Growth and change

By 1945, when World War II ended, Australians had become more aware of their neighbouring countries in the Far East, and also of the United States as a powerful protector in a future war. They realized that they were a tiny population in an immense island-continent, and that both the population and the economy had grown only slowly since federation. So they decided to

began in the 1960s with enormous growth and change in the suburbs and in the City. The population really began to boom, with the help of the families of the 'new' Australians, and the suburbs spread even further from the city centre. At the same time, the economy was boosted by the discovery of minerals (such as iron and nickel) all over the empty continent.

One obvious symbol of Sydney's new energy is that bold, extravagant project, the Sydney Opera House. The building was opened in 1973 by Queen Elizabeth II (who is still Queen of Australia) at a time when both Sydney and Australia were becoming more confident of their own non-British identity, and of their Asian-Pacific place in the world.

During the 1970s the face of Sydney was altered by giant office buildings in the City, tower blocks round the harbour's edge, and new expressways. The people of Sydney revelled in the excitement of it all, but many were alarmed by the suddenness and speed of what was happening. Groups of residents formed to protect harbourside suburbs. Trade union workers were able to prevent the destruction and redevelopment of certain areas of old, familiar Sydney and the pace of change is slower now.

Below: Sydney Opera House under construction in the 1960's. In 1955 there was an international architectural competition to design an opera house for Bennelong Point, the jutting promontory which forms one side of Sydney Cove. The brilliant 'shell' design of the Dane Jørn Utzon was chosen even though, at this point, his idea was no more than a drawing. This picture shows the final stages of the construction of the concrete shells, after the engineers had triumphed over what seemed impossible problems. The size and daring design of the building suit the harbour perfectly and reflect the optimism of modern Sydney.

invite great numbers of Britons and Europeans to settle in Australia. This decision was to have a far-reaching effect on the Australian way of life. Perhaps one third of the 100 000 who came every year settled in Sydney but the newcomers were no longer 90 per cent British. Sydney life was enriched with the cultures of Greeks, Italians, Germans, Yugoslavs and many others.

The present phase of the history of Sydney

Left: Manly beach in the late 1920's. This is not the famous ocean beach, but the shark-proof harbour beach, which lies just on the other side of the North Head peninsula. All the Pacific beaches have been discovered now, as well as the delights of surfing, but this picture reminds us that a more formal, less boisterous kind of sea bathing was once very popular.

The harbour

Perhaps as long as two million years ago, the sea level rose and many river valleys along the mountainous east coast of Australia were flooded. The greatest of them became Sydney harbour. The two mighty bluffs which stand on either side of the entrance are called the Heads. They must once have been part of a high ridge of hills similar to the Blue Mountains, 50 kilometres inland.

Nearly 200 years ago, Governor Phillip reported back to London on the nature of this harbour. He could not disguise the excitement he felt on his 'discovery' of "the finest harbour in the world, in which a thousand [ships] of the line may ride in perfect security."

Yet even more remarkable than the sheer size of this haven is its variety – the hundreds of inlets, bays, coves, creeks, peninsulars and headlands, the endless picturesque twists and turns. In fact, Sydney harbour is made up of three more or less distinct bodies of water: Middle Harbour, which branches off northwards, near the Heads; Port Jackson, at the head of which Phillip sited his Sydney Town; and beyond it the narrowing Parramatta River, a reminder of the original valley.

The highest ground is on the north side, while much of the land between the south side of the harbour and wide, shallow Botany Bay was rolling sandhills at the time the Europeans first arrived.

This great harbour, then, both unites and separates Sydney. The famous Bridge of course links City and north shore and dramatically changed the pattern of Sydney life when it was opened in 1932. Together with the Gladesville Bridge of 1964, the second bridge to span the harbour, it has allowed Sydney to become a city of car drivers.

The harbour as a pleasureground

At weekends it seems as if everybody is out on the harbour in yachts – from dinghys and catamarans to schooners – and in launches and power-boats of all kinds. There are marinas and mooring places for many thousands of boats in the dozens of bays and inlets around the shore.

Right: There are lots of fish in the harbour and hundreds of places to fish from: by open waters, in the many creeks and inlets, or from a boat – your own, or a hired one.

Left: Watson's Bay, one of the best-known harbour beaches and famous for its sea-food restaurant. It is just inside South Head, a peaceful distance from the City skyscrapers. There is a netted enclosure nearby for shark-free swimming.

Below: An aerial view looking east to the Heads and the Pacific: north shore on the left, City and docks on the right. You can see clearly why the Harbour Bridge is needed.

Though open to the ocean only at the Heads, the harbour has been shark-infested ever since the early whalers threw their waste into the water, so its tranquil beaches are protected by barriers and nets. It has a number of islands, which are the knobby peaks of drowned ridges. They were once fearful places of imprisonment but are now picnic spots. Beneath the glittering blue water the bottom of the harbour is said to be littered with rubbish!

The harbour at work

Every day, office workers journey to and from the City in harbour ferries which cross the tracks of cruise liners, container ships, freighters and warships from the naval dockyards. Residents in harbourside suburbs catch glimpses of its waters at the end of the street and hear the fog-horns on misty mornings.

Development and conservation

Harbourside homes are in great demand and in many places tall blocks of 'home units' crowd the shore. People protested that the essential character of the winding shoreline was being destroyed by the new buildings. Now strict planning controls limit them, and at the same time a number of privately owned footpaths by the shore have been restored to the public.

Perhaps more than ever before the harbour belongs to the people. Old warehouses have new identities as waterfront theatres and restaurants. On New Year's Eve, thousands gather for open-air parties in harbourside parks and houses – and on boats on the water – to watch the spectacular fireworks display at midnight.

The suburbs

In the big Australian cities, the part called the City is where you find offices, banks, government buildings, theatres and big department stores; the suburbs are where everyone lives. There are old, crowded inner suburbs, and newer suburbs of modern, one-storey houses spreading further and further out from the central area.

Inner suburbs

The inner suburbs cluster round the city centre. In Sydney these were the first suburbs, and they grew up from the 1870s. They housed the first office and factory workers and their families, mostly in two- and three-storey terraces. Some, like Redfern, turned into slums, until massive housing blocks were built in the 1960s and 70s. Others, like neighbouring Paddington, are now fashionable and expensive places to live. Just in time, a new generation of Sydney people moved in and restored the 19th century houses. They were attracted not only by the charm and elegance of the old buildings but also by a different style of life from that of the newer suburbs. Close to the City and harbour, there are shops and restaurants around every corner and though not much space for cars, not a great need either.

Above: Sydney suburbia, leafy, comfortable and peaceful. These houses were built between the two World Wars.

Below: A street in hilly Paddington. These 19th century terraces with their beautiful cast-iron 'Paddington lace' balconies and railings, are now fashionable places to live.

A lot of these 19th century buildings are divided into flats. In fact Sydney has many more flat-dwellers, or people who live in 'home units', than any other Australian city. In some harbourside and inner suburbs more than half the people live in home units, whether in simple two-storey buildings or in luxurious new tower blocks.

Outer suburbs

Even so, the majority of the people of Sydney live quite differently; in spacious family houses with their own front garden, back garden with a patio and possibly a swimming pool, and a garage for one or two cars and perhaps a small boat. Corner shops have survived, thanks to immigrant families taking them over. In older suburbs the local high street shopping centres have free car parks. But even here families shop more and more in the huge new regional shopping centres designed for the family and the car.

The spread of the suburbs began in the harbourside areas. Then it followed the railways, south to Botany Bay, north over the Bridge along the bushland ridge of the north shore, and west and southwest to Parramatta and beyond.

Western suburbs

Public transport could no longer keep pace when the rate of the spread speeded up dramatically in the 1960s, creating many new

outer suburbs. This happened because the children born in the 'baby boom' years after World War II, and also the children of new immigrant families, had grown up. Now they were marrying and expecting to have their own new houses in the Australian style. Thousands of houses were built almost overnight and couples often moved in before the electricity and sewerage had been connected. The new suburban streets raced ahead of these basic services (and of schools and shops too) and swallowed up the great market-garden plains west of Sydney, leaving the harbour and City far behind.

The terrific energy which established these western suburbs has made them into the new heart of working Sydney. The whole area, with its factories, workshops and refineries, is mainly flat, treeless and remote from the water. It can feel mercilessly exposed in the summer sun.

Yet there is no looking back over the shoulder to the glamour of central and harbourside Sydney. Here, in the 'capitals' of the area, such as Liverpool or Blacktown, the people – mostly young, and of many national origins – feel very much at the centre of life in the Sydney of today.

Above: The interior of one of the new suburban shopping centres. These provide not only every kind of shop and department store under one roof, but also cafés, exhibitions, and play areas.

Left: Suburban shopping streets like this have suffered with the development of the regional shopping centre. But they still meet the needs of the local people with the usual shops and services, and in fact they now also provide supermarkets and car parks. The big, almost American-style, cars (and taxi), the wide awnings for shade from the sun, and the overhead telephone and electricity lines are all common in Australian cities.

The beach

It could be said that Sydneysiders do not yet enjoy their harbour to the full. But the Pacific beaches are another matter. Here, for all but a few months of the year, the people of Sydney certainly make the most of sun, sea and sand.

Famous beaches

The harbour has its beaches, sheltered and often very pretty, but 'the beach' usually means the string of surf beaches which stretches over 50 kilometres along the Pacific coast from Broken Bay, north of Sydney, to Botany Bay. Here is a roll-call of the best-known beaches, names which call up the very spirit of Sydney: north of the Heads are Palm Beach, Avalon, Mona Vale, Narrabeen, Collaroy, Dee Why, Curl Curl, Manly; and to the south are Bondi, Clovelly, Coogee, Maroubra, Cronulla.

At the beach

On Saturdays and Sundays in summer almost everyone goes to the beach. Many go by car; others who live nearer go on bikes or on foot or, if they come from the inland suburbs, by train or bus. During the week, parents take their pre-school children in the morning before the sun gets too hot; keen surfers go before work or school; many visit

Below: Typical Sydney beach scene. The many umbrellas provide welcome shade from the sun and make the beach a comfortable place for the family to relax and laze away the day together. Because there are so many beaches – one after the other up and down the coast, each with its own character – they are never too crowded. Sydney has a high rainfall but it comes in heavy, almost tropical, bursts so the sunshine is seldom interrupted for long.

Above: Every beach is patrolled by life savers. Some stay close to the water and keep in touch with others who look out with binoculars from the high vantage-point of the club house.

Below: Lunch break for fish and chips – you can practically live on the beach! Two members of this family are wearing shirts to protect them from sunburn – as are several of the people in the water.

the beach at the end of the day when the sun has lost its sting; and at lunchtime, beaches near the City, like Bondi, are crowded with office workers. Radio weather bulletins keep everyone up to date on conditions of both weather and surf.

All the beaches are open to everyone and you can sit or lie wherever you choose. The easy-going Sydney way of life is seen at its best here. Teenagers find the beach a perfect place to meet and sit around, among the general crowd but at the same time apart

from it. Young children play in the sand and paddle at the frothy edge of the surf, or learn to swim in a sheltered pool at the rocky end of the beach. Old people snooze in chairs under big umbrellas. The majority lie and sunbake in between cooling-off spells in the water. These days the ice-box packed with food and drink will not be the only thing shielded from the burning sun. People know about the risk of skin cancer from too much sun and are happy to go along with the recent health slogan, "Slip on a shirt, slap on a hat, slop on some cream."

Meanwhile, life-savers patrol the swimming area between the flags, where hundreds of people are diving in and out of the crashing surf, and body surfing. They are on the look-out for swimmers being dragged out by the treacherous undertow of the waves, and for sharks – bells are rung to call everybody from the water if one appears.

Surfers and fishermen

Beyond the flags the board riders practise their skills, hoping for the perfect wave to take them into the beach. On cliffs at either end of the beach, especially north and south of Bondi, fishermen perch on rocks above the foaming waves. Behind the beach there are shops and stalls for cold drinks, hamburgers, ice-cream, sun hats and sun-tan oil. There may also be changing rooms and a lawn of thick tropical grass. And of course there is always the car park.

Above: A surf carnival. Watched by thousands of people, these events are held at the main beaches throughout the surfing season – roughly October to March. They consist of a series of competitions between surf life-saving clubs, including the traditional march-past pictured here. There are life-boat races through the waves and back, and similar races for individual swimmers ending with a sprint up the beach. In the rescue and resuscitation competition, clubs are marked not only for speed but also for efficiency and correct techniques.

Growing up in Sydney

Australians live very little in the past and very much in the present. When they look to the future it is only to think optimistically about their children. Their way of life is shaped by the family. That is the reason for the suburban houses and gardens, the airy modern schools, the shopping centres, the cars. This is especially so in Sydney where the pattern of family life is built around the simple pleasures provided by the sun, the harbour, the beaches, the sports grounds and the natural parkland.

Early in life a child grows familiar with the beach and the sound of the surf. If they live far from the beach, mother will take the children to the big open-air neighbourhood swimming baths where they soon learn to swim. At school, sports and games – from hockey to scuba-diving to chess – are important from the start. At home, the family regularly enjoys a barbecue meal on the back patio by the small swimming pool that many houses have for the younger children. Inside at night, family life is dominated by television, with its mixture of Australian, American and British programmes.

Below: Not all growing up in Sydney takes place outdoors, in the sun or on the water. Scuba-diving may be taught in schools, but, much more commonly, so are art, drama, dance and music. There are youth orchestras and groups throughout Sydney. At this summer music camp, young people from many different schools learn orchestral playing under experienced conductors.

Above: Proud members of a surf life-saving club. Despite many new attractions – from windsurfing to dune-buggy riding – this traditional part of Sydney life is still very popular with teenagers. The work of patrolling the beaches is unpaid and many hours of training are needed to make life savers. They must be very strong swimmers, capable of getting out quickly beyond the big waves and supporting an unconscious swimmer. The boys pictured here carry the oars of a life-saving boat. These traditional boats have been replaced by motor boats and surf skis in rescue work, but are still raced in surf carnivals.

The design of the giant shells had to be altered to fit in the theatrical machinery, and their construction in concrete became a colossal engineering problem. The architect, the Dane Jørn Utzon, resigned from the project and the costs soared to undreamed-of heights. Sydney raised the money by holding state lotteries, and the engineers worked out how to build the shells. In the end, because of a series of political squabbles and planning mistakes, the performance of opera was relegated to the second of the three main halls which will never be quite large enough. The main hall is a magnificent venue for symphony concerts and the like but cannot regularly stage opera itself.

The basic shape of the building is so marvellous, resembling white billowing sails on the harbour or a pair of settling swans, that none of this seems to matter. And the Opera House has become the cultural and artistic centre of Sydney.

The Rocks

Similarly, the new Rocks development fulfils a function in the life of Sydney which, before its completion, no one could be sure existed. A hundred years ago, in the days when Sydney was a rip-roaring port for ships and sailors from all over the world, the Rocks – the rocky point of land on which one end of the Bridge now sits – was the centre of all the dock-side life. Behind the docks and wharves was an insanitary rabbit-warren of houses and lanes, full of taverns, gambling dens and gangs of 'larrikins'. (The leader of one of these gangs of toughs, Young Griffo, became a world boxing champion.)

On the rocky land above were the large and stately homes of rich ship-owners and merchants. When the Harbour Bridge was built these were all demolished, but the smaller houses on the slopes below remained. In recent years the old docks and warehouses were abandoned for the new container docks a couple of bays beyond. As land by the harbour had become immensely valuable by the 1970s, there was great pressure to sweep everything away and build luxury tower blocks and conference centres.

Instead, conservationists won the day. This remnant of old Sydney has been saved and key buildings adapted to new uses as restaurants, craft centres, shops and museums.

Right: Craft shops in a corner of the restored Rocks area, almost in the shadow of the Bridge (and within earshot of its thundering traffic). The rough and tumble, rascally Rocks neighbourhood of old is long gone, but the buildings and the steep lanes have been preserved.

Below: A school party visits Cadman's Cottage, Sydney's oldest surviving dwelling, in the heart of the Rocks area. Built in 1816 for the governor's boat crew, it is now a maritime museum, one of several museums in the Rocks. As is usual in Sydney, these school-children wear a uniform.

The City and the Cross

Governor Phillip's primitive little prison settlement at Sydney Cove is now, two hundred years later, a cluster of gleaming skyscrapers. Its narrow grid of streets was laid out by 1817, in Macquarie's time. The original source of fresh water, called the Tank Stream, once divided the quarters of officers on one side and soldiers and convicts on the other. It has long been underground, and Pitt Street now marks its course.

The City

The City, with its town hall, government house, big stores and luxury shops, art gallery, museums, botanical gardens, central railway station and underground line has always been the centre of Sydney and the place where most people worked. But over the years industry left the City area and fewer people came into town to shop, preferring the convenience and lavish amenities of the suburban shopping centres.

However, since the 1960s, the City has been revived. New building has transformed it from a solid, dignified, 19th century city, no more than five storeys high, to one of startling height and modernity. It has become an exciting and prosperous international financial centre, and the mighty mineral companies have attracted thousands of new workers to their towering headquarters.

At street level much has changed too. People can relax from the rush and noise in shaded plazas or, if they wish, at the outdoor tables of the new cafés and restaurants.

Above: The City from Circular Quay, the original anchorage and landing spot of the first settlers, two hundred years ago. Cruise liners berth here (on the right), while the quay is lined with wharves for ferries. The one in the picture is a traditional ferry. There are also hydrofoils which make the 11 kilometre journey to Manly, for instance, in 20 minutes. An elevated expressway squeezes through, funneling cars from the Bridge to the eastern suburbs.

Left: Martin Place has always been the centre of the City. It is now closed to traffic and part of it has been redesigned, and renamed Martin Plaza. There are flower stalls, a large fountain, lots of seats and an area for lunch-time entertainment as shown in this picture.

Sophisticated underground shopping centres have been built, insulated from the summer heat as well as from the noise of traffic. At the same time, elegant arcades and ornate market buildings of the last century have been restored to their former glory. Most important, people are returning to the City to live, as old buildings such as warehouses are converted into home units, and new blocks of flats are built.

There are still hundreds of thousands of Sydneysiders who do not work in the City. In fact, nowadays many people hardly ever go there, as work, sport and entertainment are all available in the suburbs. Yet the City is the glittering focus of the new prosperity that Sydney enjoys – and nearby is 'the Cross', which is anything but suburban.

The Cross

King's Cross is about two kilometres east of the City, beyond down-at-heel Woolloomooloo and short of the exclusive harbourside suburbs that stretch to South Head. It is the place where sailors on shore leave have always headed for, certain that something would be going on at any time of the day or night.

Though much has changed in King's Cross, its lively, cosmopolitan atmosphere remains. A massive hotel and shopping development has recently been built on the edge of the area, but King's Cross escaped the complete

redevelopment that threatened it in the 1970s. It is still a crowded jumble of all sorts of bars and clubs and restaurants. Anything can happen in King's Cross, they say, and it usually does. On New Year's Eve, the rowdiest party in Sydney takes place here, and the streets are jammed solid with revellers from far and wide.

The new spectacular high-rise City, together with low-rise, never-sleeping King's Cross – as well as the Opera House and the redeveloped Rocks area – give the people of Sydney today a real City to use and look towards from the comfort of their suburban homes.

Above: A taxi-rank in King's Cross. This garish, cosmopolitan heart of Sydney never closes for fun and entertainment.

Below: The Strand Arcade in the City, restored to its original 19th-century splendour as part of the campaign to bring shoppers back to the centre of Sydney.

The bush and the national parks

The suburbs may seem endless but in fact Sydney has clearly defined boundaries. To the east, of course, the Pacific Ocean stretches a quarter of the world away to the west coast of America. To the west the Blue Mountains still present a formidable barrier and have been declared a national park, where new building is severely restricted. To the north great tracts of beautiful wild bushland on either side of Broken Bay and the Hawkesbury River have also been protected as national parks. And on the coast to the south of Botany Bay there is another (the first) national park. These parks do not completely ring Sydney but they are the third element of the great outdoors that the city is so richly blessed with. After the harbour and the beaches, comes the bush. No other city in Australia has such easy access to wild bushland.

The first settlers and the later squatters could find no use for these tracts of neighbouring country. The land was inaccessible and covered with thick woodland. It was difficult to clear, so has remained unspoiled and is now protected.

Above: Boiling a 'billy' of tea watched by a native bird – this one is a galah. For a day, or for a week or more, the city-dweller can return to the bush and live like the old pioneers. On days of very high fire risk no fires of any kind are allowed in these bushland national parks.

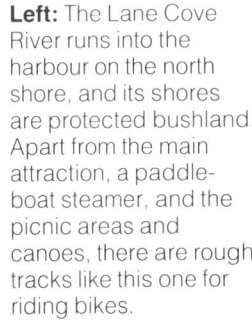

Left: The Lane Cove River runs into the harbour on the north shore, and its shores are protected bushland. Apart from the main attraction, a paddle-boat steamer, and the picnic areas and canoes, there are rough tracks like this one for riding bikes.

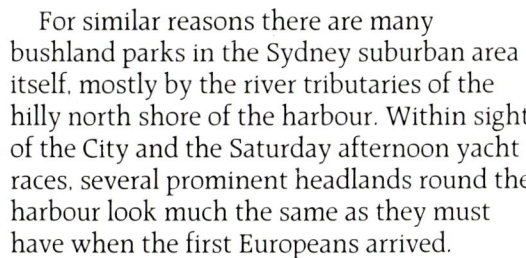

Left: This bush walker is equipped with everything he needs for exploring the wild bushland in one of the huge national parks just beyond the Sydney suburban area – bushland unchanged for countless thousands of years.

Below: The national parks are what you make them. As well as rugged bushland, the parks contain cool leafy dells by rivers and creeks. Here, in the Royal National Park to the south of Sydney, a family of Lebanese Australians enjoys a day of complete relaxation.

For similar reasons there are many bushland parks in the Sydney suburban area itself, mostly by the river tributaries of the hilly north shore of the harbour. Within sight of the City and the Saturday afternoon yacht races, several prominent headlands round the harbour look much the same as they must have when the first Europeans arrived.

In recent years, as Australians have become surer of their own identity as Australians rather than transplanted Europeans, they have 'discovered' the peculiar beauty of their own country. In particular they have discovered the bush and bush walking. The bush has usually been described as strange and mysterious and timeless because it is so different from European woods and forests. Australians no longer bother with such descriptions. They have adopted the bush at last as native and natural. They have set about protecting as much as they can that has survived clearance.

Bush walkers

The ever-necessary family car is provided with access to the bush and parking, but that is all. The bush is preserved for the unique native trees, flowers, animals, birds and insects, then, and only then, for bush walkers. In summer bush walkers make for beaches and other swimming places in the park, following maps provided by the information centre. There are tracks and routes for all ages. Mostly people walk to enjoy the beauties of the bush, learning to recognize birds and wild flowers and resting from the noise and rush of a big modern city.

Bushfires

The combination of cars, people and bushland can be highly dangerous. A cigarette butt, a carelessly lit fire or even a discarded bottle lying in dry grass can set off terrible fires. In places the bush penetrates to the very heart of Sydney, and even suburban houses are sometimes threatened by bushfires, especially if a harsh north wind blows at the height of summer, when the dry bush air is heavy with eucalyptus sap. Deciding to build a house in the beautiful mountains on the outskirts of Sydney is a little like settling on the slope of a volcano. The fire-spotting planes are ever-vigilant but neither they nor the brave firefighting teams can ever eliminate bushfires.

New and old Australians

Below: This mother and son originally came from Italy. She may never speak much English, but he is a confident young Italian Sydneysider. They live in one of the older suburbs where there are Italian shops, clubs, churches and newspapers. The Italians are one of the largest single ethnic groups in Sydney.

Many Italians go into business as building contractors, and some become enormously successful business tycoons. Many sons and daughters of poor parents do well at school and go to university.

Sydney has changed dramatically since the 1960s. This is partly because of the new mineral wealth, but it is also because of the huge influx of 'new' Australians. Since the end of World War II, hundreds of thousands of working people have arrived from Europe and the Far East, and the old British-Australian way of life – which was set in its simple routines – has been greatly enriched by many different cultures. Sydney life is more interesting and varied than it used to be and the newcomers – especially those from Mediterranean countries – have even taught the Australians how to live more stylishly outdoors and helped them to discover the food and cooking of other countries.

'New' Australians

To begin with, a newly arrived family, after a brief stay at a migrant hostel, will head for the places where most others of their nationality live and have set up shops and clubs. For instance, the Italians colonized Leichhardt, an old suburb not far from the City, where factory workers used to live. The other big ethnic community, the Greeks, settled first in nearby Newtown. But they revived this old area so successfully that smart young executives now live there. The centre of Greek Sydney has moved down the railway line to Marrickville. Vietnamese refugees set up shops and businesses in the far western suburb of Cabramatta. The City itself has a large traditional Chinatown and even a Spanish Town.

But the immigrants quickly become Australian. Their children go to local schools and when they grow up they buy houses wherever they can afford to, like any other young people in Sydney.

Two things make this possible – the openness and equality of Australian society and the high level of prosperity. The new Australians have contributed to this prosperity, just as those who set up the immigration programme intended. No one could have foreseen, though, how much Australia would be changed in the process. At the time of World War II, 95 per cent of Australians were descended from people who came from Britain or Ireland. By now that percentage is more like 50.

Left: A swimming instructor and class. The Asian children are from the latest wave of immigrants to enrich multi-cultural Sydney. They are refugees from recent wars in South-East Asia and understandably look slightly bewildered in this new, happy-go-lucky atmosphere. But the Sydney way of life is not difficult to catch on to and they will be encouraged to join in.

Below: A picnic Yugoslav-style on the grass under the Norfolk Island pine trees that line the esplanades behind many Sydney beaches. Many ethnic groups use the beach in this way, creating a lively new blend of cultures.

In recent years, more and more immigrants have come from Asian countries, especially Vietnam, Malaysia and Indonesia. They now make up at least a third of the total number of immigrants each year. By the year 2000, Australia may well be truly a part of South-East Asia.

Aborigines

Of course all Australians are new Australians – apart from the original inhabitants, the Aborigines. Deprived of their land by successive generations of settlers, this noble ancient hunting and gathering people have never become part of urban or suburban life. Those in Sydney live mostly in run-down inner suburban Redfern – often poor and dispirited – and remain apart from the rest of society.

Recently, leaders have emerged to speak for the Aborigines and there is more awareness of the terrible wrongs done to them in the past. People are beginning to appreciate their ancient culture and to recognize their land rights. In Sydney the National Aborigines Week every July features a march from Redfern to the town hall, and the government sponsors the travelling Aboriginal and Islanders Dance Company. But there is still a much greater gap to bridge than there is between European or Asian immigrants and British-Australian culture.

Right: A corner of the main fish market in dockside Pyrmont, near the City. Australians have always eaten far more meat than fish. But now the influence of immigrant cultures has made the people of Sydney more aware of the great wealth of fish and marine life at their doorstep. Here young Vietnamese women, in their element in this traditional market stall, sell Pacific prawns, famous for their size.

Festivals and fun

As Sydney grows, and becomes more cosmopolitan, the people of Sydney see it less and less as a kind of British or American city. They have learned to adapt customs and ideas from many cultures to their own climate, geography and way of life – and to come up with ideas of their own. For example, businessmen no longer dress according to a British idea of formality. They live by the sunny Pacific and the weather is often hot and sticky, so tailored shorts and long white socks plus collar and tie are now common wear. Indeed, everyone wears shorts whenever possible, and generally dress is light and casual – as free and easy as the climate and the people.

When it comes to enjoying themselves, Sydneysiders take advantage of their surroundings. In a city which loves its live theatre there are now open-air, harbourside theatres. Parkland everywhere is being changed from the formal European kind, which dries up in the Australian summer, and planted with thousands of native trees. The parkland is also being landscaped with new paths, car parks, playgrounds and barbecues.

Above all, in the new multi-cultural Sydney, eating out is a big part of life. Eating and drinking used to mean red meat and beer. While the meat (and the beer) are still

plentiful, there is now an almost overwhelming choice and range of food and styles of cooking. You can eat Lebanese style one night, French another; Chinese, Italian, Spanish, Vietnamese and so on, in modestly priced restaurants where people can bring their own wine. For cheap and 'fast' food, pizza parlours can be found everywhere, vying with traditional fish and chip shops and chains of American hamburger bars.

The people of Sydney, it has been said, take their fun seriously and do not allow things like work to get in the way of it.

Above: Christmas dinner in Sydney. Despite the steamy heat of the Sydney summer, many households serve the traditional roast turkey and plum pudding. Christmas is even more of a hectic time in Australia than it is in Europe or America, for it coincides with the end of school and the start of the summer holiday.

Left: Luna Park, Sydney's famous fun-fair, has blared out its noise and colours from its harbour site below the north end of the Harbour Bridge for over fifty years. It is a short ferry ride from Circular Quay, and after recent restoration it is now as popular as it ever was. The most exciting (and terrifying) rides are on the eleven storey high ferris wheel, and on the roller-coaster. The children's section has scaled-down versions of the big rides as well as a BMX bike track.

The Easter Show

Until recently the one big festival of the year was the Royal Easter Show, where judging of livestock and displays of farm equipment came second to all the side shows, the candy floss and the sample bags of sweets and toys. The Show is still a great favourite, and the last day is a half-price 'Kids' Day'.

The Festival of Sydney

There is now, however, a real full-blown Festival of Sydney. It takes place in the City, beginning on New Year's Eve with fireworks and celebrations at the Opera House, and lasts the whole of January. On Australia Day (26 January) a grand parade winds through the City, and throughout the month there are many kinds of cultural events and entertainments for children and adults. Best of all, perhaps, are the open-air concerts in the Domain. At these, a huge audience sits and lies on the grass under the stars, listening to symphony concerts, jazz, opera or rock bands.

Other festivals

The harbour holds its own unofficial festival every Boxing Day, when hundreds of boats surround the competitors in the Sydney to Hobart yacht race. The big yachts sail out to the Heads and the ocean at the start of their race to Hobart in Tasmania. The beach has its festivals too – the traditional competitive surf life-saving carnivals which still attract thousands of spectators regularly through the long summer. Other local festivals abound. Manly's Summer Festival is based on surf and water sports, and they also have a Jazz Festival in October. In outer suburban Blacktown, the City Festival spreads over two June weekends, with as many as 100 000 spectactors at the big parade.

Night-time fun

For entertainment and fun at night Sydneysiders love their pubs and clubs. The biggest and best by far are the rugby league clubs, financed by poker-machines – 'the pokies' or one-armed bandits which are unique to Sydney. The biggest clubs are incredibly wealthy and have built enormous headquarters. These pleasure palaces provide squash courts, swimming pools, indoor cricket (the latest craze), saunas, gymnasiums, cinemas, libraries and of course restaurants, bars, discotheques and live entertainment from famous performers. Poker machines, or those who feed them with money, pay for all this, so membership fees are very low. For the children of members the clubs put on all sorts of free entertainment, outings and sport.

Above: A ferry-boat race on the harbour during the Festival of Sydney. These sedate craft normally carry up to 1500 passengers to and from work each day.

There are other races that take place on the harbour during the Festival – even one for zany home-made craft.

The Blue Mountains

In its early days, the convict colony of Sydney was itself imprisoned on the coast by the impenetrable barrier of the Blue Mountains, 50 kilometres inland. This high tableland is a maze of towering rocky bluffs, plummeting ravines and dense bushland. For a quarter of a century it defeated the many heroic and often heart-breaking attempts to find a way over to what was hoped would be green pastures, or possibly an inland sea. Finally, in 1813, a party led by the adventurous explorers Blaxland, Wentworth and Lawson succeeded by following the ridges instead of seeking non-existent valley passes. They were rewarded with the discovery of vast grassy plains on the other side – limitless grazing lands and wheat fields for the rapidly expanding colony. Similar heroic achievements followed – a small gang of convicts built 160 kilometres of road across the mountain wilderness in six months, and 50 years later the first railway was constructed.

Mountain retreats

In these beautiful but daunting mountains, settlement is limited to a few towns on the road through. The biggest town, Katoomba, was originally a quarry site for the first railway embankments.

A certain amount of timber was felled in the mountains, but their main use was as a retreat from the summer heat. The genteel and stately guest houses and hotels of the Blue Mountains are now enjoying a revival as Sydney people discover how restful such old-fashioned ways can be. Today, families are building second homes high in the secluded bush. These are weekend retreats back to nature, away from the noise and pollution of the city. In fact since the electrification of the railway many people can now live in the Blue Mountains and commute to the City daily.

Tourism

For a long time a number of spectacular bluffs and viewpoints have been popular beauty spots. Now that the Blue Mountains are protected as a national park, access roads and picnic areas have been carefully introduced.

Best of all, a network of rough tracks has been established for bush walkers, making it

Above: The most famous landmark in the Blue Mountains, the Three Sisters near Katoomba. The blue haze of the mountains is broken regularly by lines of eroded cliffs such as those you can see in the background. These were the terrible barriers which the early explorers kept encountering.

Left: If you go a little way off the beaten track, you soon find yourself in the midst of a tangle of ancient scrub and tumbling waters.

Above: Viewpoints like this one allow car-driving tourists to keep well clear of bush tracks and hard walking – and leave the lone bush walkers in peace. From here, tourists can see the famous Three Sisters.

Below: The Scenic Skyway is suspended 300 metres above the valley floor. From the cable car you can appreciate fully the courage and achievements of the first explorers and railway builders.

possible for enthusiasts to penetrate and explore the ancient bushland for days at a time.

Katoomba is the flourishing tourist centre for all this. From here you can take a ride on the cable-suspended Scenic Skyway, 300 metres above the neighbouring valley, as well as on "the world's steepest railway". Further west, an old, zig-zag section of the railway has been restored for pleasure use.

Development

Not all of the Blue Mountains area is protected, it seems, for approval has recently been given to develop the small town of Leura. The development of a new town in the midst of this unique wilderness will be fiercely opposed by conservationists. They argue that it is the wrong solution to the problem of the sprawling suburbs.

The future

The people of Sydney have welcomed the world of the late 20th century with typical zest. No longer isolated and provincial, Sydney is now one of the great cities of the world. Yet although still insulated by distance from many of the difficulties of the Western world, Sydney cannot escape the problems of pollution and suburban sprawl.

A brown haze of chemical smog regularly covers the city. Massive sewerage outlets are sited dangerously close to many of the famous beaches – the surfing forecasts sometimes warn against swimming at all at certain beaches because of polluted water. More and more roads are needed for more and more cars as the suburbs stretch further than anyone could have imagined possible.

So far it just about works, and the temptation to believe that it always will, as long as the sun keeps shining, is very strong. Even being unemployed in Sydney is not so bad as it is in most other cities, and the climate and beaches can make it almost pleasant at times.

There is a common Australian expression "She'll be right," meaning, "Relax, don't make a fuss, things will turn out all right." But the easy optimism summed up in this phrase cannot guarantee prosperity. In the end, Sydney's wealth depends on the changeable world-wide need for Australia's primary products: wheat and wool, and minerals such as iron ore and nickel.

The expanding workforce, boosted by immigrants, is being directed towards new industries, like the giant refinery by Botany Bay which is based on Australia's new-found off-shore oil. Meanwhile everyone is happy while they share in the 'good life'. Will it still be as good, though, if Sydney forms one continuous urban area with its industrial neighbour Woolongong down the coast? (The national park only partially blocks the way.) How far can you spread the happy-go-lucky spirit of Sydney which comes from being close to the harbour and the beaches?

Some of the basic problems have been solved by moving factories and shops out to the suburban 'regions'. (Botany Bay has been developed as a second big shipping port.) Lead-free petrol will cut down much of the smog. Public transport is being given more attention too – the Eastern Suburbs Railway was finally built after much delay, and there is a move to revive some of the old ferry routes in an attempt to reduce the number of cars in the city.

The larger problem lies beyond the control of Sydney itself. Perhaps a nationwide plan to develop inland cities and towns will be the only answer to the unlimited expansion, and eventual stifling, of Sydney.

Below: Passengers leaving a harbour ferry. Most public transport in Sydney is run by one organization, in order to solve the many problems created by the harbour. The Urban Transit Authority hopes to reduce road traffic by using the harbour itself.

Before the Harbour Bridge was built, over 40 million passengers a year were carried by the ferries (which started to operate in 1854, when the Manly Ferry service began). As less than a quarter of this number uses the ferries today, there is plenty of scope for more ferry routes and many more passengers on the existing ones.

Above: The Harbour Bridge, seen from north Sydney. Huge new expressways have been built to speed the flow of traffic across the harbour and to and from the City. This has attracted more traffic of course. Thousands of commuters now park their cars in north Sydney and catch a bus or train across.

Left: View of suburban Wooloomooloo. The future may look like this all over inner Sydney: more railways and new high-density housing in a style inspired by the old terraced houses.

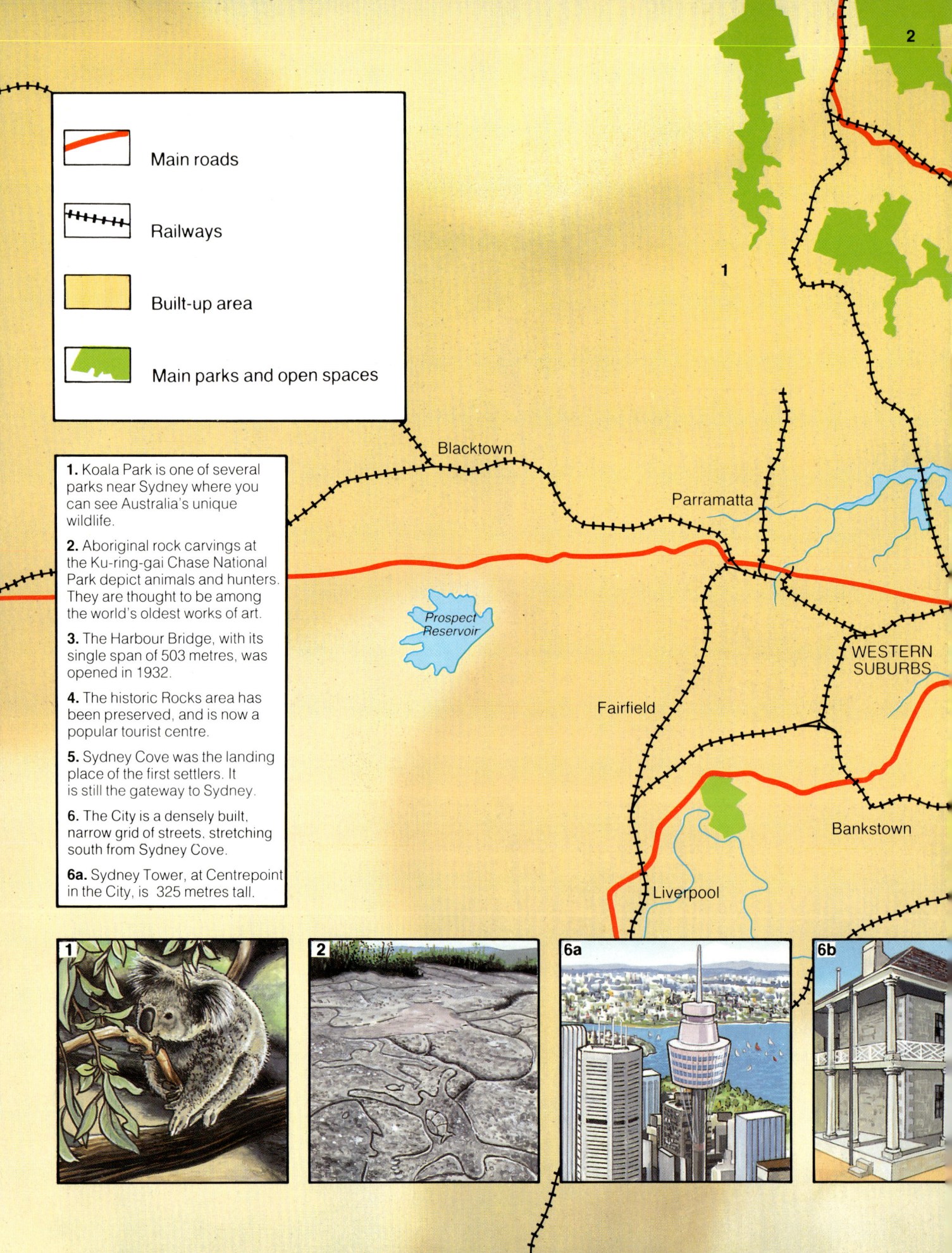

1

Legend

Main roads

Railways

Built-up area

Main parks and open spaces

1. Koala Park is one of several parks near Sydney where you can see Australia's unique wildlife.

2. Aboriginal rock carvings at the Ku-ring-gai Chase National Park depict animals and hunters. They are thought to be among the world's oldest works of art.

3. The Harbour Bridge, with its single span of 503 metres, was opened in 1932.

4. The historic Rocks area has been preserved, and is now a popular tourist centre.

5. Sydney Cove was the landing place of the first settlers. It is still the gateway to Sydney.

6. The City is a densely built, narrow grid of streets, stretching south from Sydney Cove.

6a. Sydney Tower, at Centrepoint in the City, is 325 metres tall.

Blacktown

Parramatta

Prospect
Reservoir

Fairfield

WESTERN
SUBURBS

Bankstown

Liverpool

1

2

6a

6b

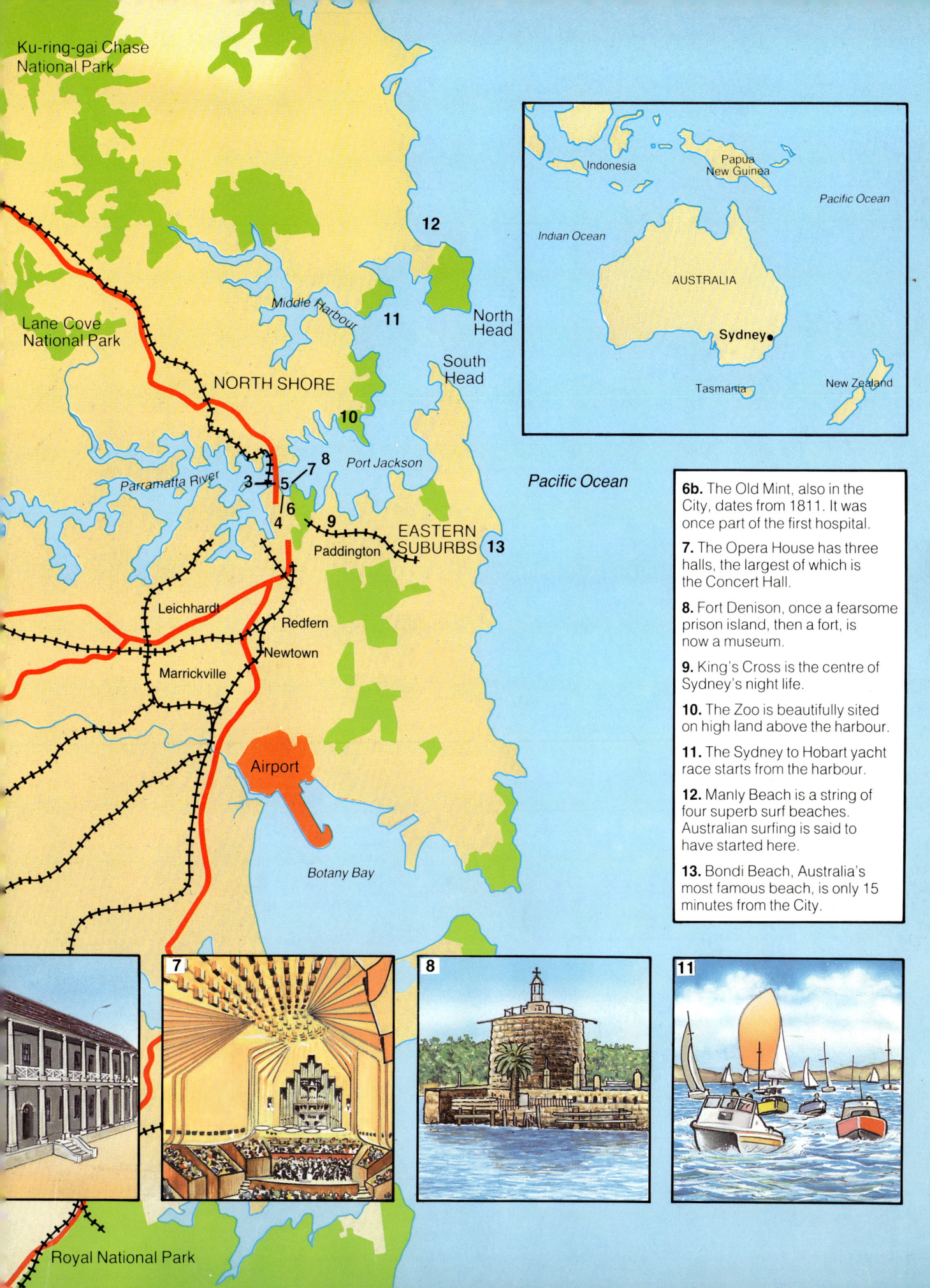

Ku-ring-gai Chase National Park

Lane Cove National Park

Middle Harbour

NORTH SHORE

Parramatta River

Leichhardt

Redfern

Newtown

Marrickville

Airport

Botany Bay

Royal National Park

12

11

North Head

South Head

10

Port Jackson

3 5 7 8

6

4

9

Paddington

EASTERN SUBURBS

13

Pacific Ocean

Indonesia

Papua New Guinea

Pacific Ocean

Indian Ocean

AUSTRALIA

Sydney

Tasmania

New Zealand

6b. The Old Mint, also in the City, dates from 1811. It was once part of the first hospital.

7. The Opera House has three halls, the largest of which is the Concert Hall.

8. Fort Denison, once a fearsome prison island, then a fort, is now a museum.

9. King's Cross is the centre of Sydney's night life.

10. The Zoo is beautifully sited on high land above the harbour.

11. The Sydney to Hobart yacht race starts from the harbour.

12. Manly Beach is a string of four superb surf beaches. Australian surfing is said to have started here.

13. Bondi Beach, Australia's most famous beach, is only 15 minutes from the City.

The language

Australians speak English with an Australian accent that varies very little between Sydney, for instance, and Perth, 2500 kilometres away on the west coast of Australia. The easy-going nature of daily life makes Australian English friendly and informal. One example of this is the way many names are given a shortened, familiar form – Paddington is known as 'Paddo', the milkman is the 'milko', mosquitoes are 'mozzies' and so on. Nick-names and slang are common in all walks of life and no one keeps their full first name. If your name cannot be shortened another name will probably be invented from your surname or your appearance (a tall person might be called 'Shorty' or a bald-headed man 'Curly').

The oldest and best-known Australian slang term is 'fair dinkum', meaning really and truly, or genuine, the real thing. Some terms have been taken up in Britain, such as the word 'whinge', meaning to complain. A typical Australian expression of enthusiasm and approval is 'ripper!'.

The Sydney Year

The Sydney year begins with the Festival of Sydney in January and ends with the start of the Sydney to Hobart yacht race on Boxing Day. In between are many other events and festivals, some of which are listed here.

January
Festival of Sydney: runs throughout January.
Manly Summer Festival.
Finals of the six-metre yacht championships.
Australia Day, 26 January, public holiday: Festival of Sydney ends.

February
School year begins.
Chinese New Year, Chinatown.

March
End of cricket season.
Royal Easter Show in Sydney showgrounds (March or April)

April
Start of rugby league season.
Anzac Day, 25 April, public holiday in memory of those who died in two World Wars.
Sydney Cup, Randwick racecourse.

May
End of first school term.
School holidays.

June
Blacktown City Festival.
Manly Winter Arts Festival.

August
August Moon Festival, Chinatown.
City to Surf Race: race for joggers from the City to Bondi Beach.

September
End of second school term.
School holidays.
Rugby league finals.
Sydney marathon.

October
Start of cricket season.
First surf carnivals.
Manly Jazz Festival.
Oktoberfest, Fairfield: German-style beer festival in western suburbs.

November
Parramatta Foundation Festival.

December
End of school year: long holidays begin.
Carols by candlelight, Thursday before Christmas, Sydney Town Hall.
Sydney to Hobart yacht race starts on Boxing Day.

Books to read

There are not many children's books about Sydney available. However, the following books will tell you more about Australia and the Australian way of life:
Australia by Elizabeth Cornelia, Macdonald Educational, 1977
Looking at Lands Australia by Robert Moore, Macdonald Educational, 1983

Aborigines of Australia by Robyn Holder, Wayland, 1985
There are many good children's novels set in Australia, including:
I Own the Racecourse by Patricia Wrightson, Puffin, 1971 and other books by the same author.
Walkabout by James Vance Marshall, Puffin, 1980. A story about an Aborigine boy and a contrast of cultures.

Index

PRINTED IN BELGIUM BY
proost
INTERNATIONAL BOOK PRODUCTION